In His Excellence

(An Usher's Manual)

By
Ronald L. Kite

NUGGET OF TRUTH MINISTRIES
P.O. Box 33110
Tulsa, OK 74153

All Scriptures used in this book are from the *King James Version* of the Bible.

ISBN 0-942847-00-8

NTM-0110

Copyright ©, 1982, by Nugget of Truth Ministries, Tulsa, Oklahoma
Printed in the United States of America.
All rights reserved.

Fourth Printing March 1992

Table Of Contents

FOREWORD 7

1 WHAT IS THE "MINISTRY OF HELPS"? 9

    Who is Involved
    What is Their Role
    Bucket Passers or Ministers
    Disciples in the Ministry of Helps

2 WHY USHERS? 17

    Ministers With a Vision
    Responsibilities of the Head Usher
    Developing an Ushers Team

3 WHAT TO LOOK FOR IN AN USHER 21

    Choosing of the Seven Deacons
    Qualities for Leadership
    Goals for Growth

4 WHY HOLD USHERS MEETINGS? 35

    Applications for Ushering
    Guidelines for an Ushers Meeting
    The Importance of "Oneness"

5 PRE-SERVICE RESPONSIBILITIES 39

    The Need to Arrive Early
    Dress Code
    The Ushers Room
    Supplies for the Ushers Room
    Transportation for the Speaker
    Purpose for a Speaker's Room

Supplies for the Speaker's Room
Security for the Speaker's Room
Handling the Speaker's Messages
Be Alert to the Speaker's Needs
Handling of Announcements
Arranging the Platform
Arranging the Seating
Special Seating Sections
Reserve Seating
Prayer Cloths (to be prayed over)
Ministry Cloths (for Healing Line)
Book Tables
Sound System, Television, and Taping
Assignments Prior to Service
Know the Layout of the Building
Counselors and Prayer Room
Ushers for Specific Locations

6 WELCOMING AND DIRECTING 58

You Are in Public Relations
Your Chief Purpose—
    Before the Service Begins
Flexibility—Last-Minute Changes
Guidelines for Seating People
Removal of Men's Hats
Things to Correct Before They Happen
Things to Handle Immediately

7 SERVICE RESPONSIBILITIES 64

You Can Help the Platform
Praise God With Your Eyes Open
What to do When the Speaker Is Late
Seating People:
    During Opening Songs
    During Worship and Praise
    Once the Service Has Begun

Removal of Crying Babies
Taking Pictures During a Service
Duties of Ushers in Back of Auditorium

8 OFFERING PROCEDURES 75

Before the Offering is Received,
   You Need to Know!
Supplies You Need Before Taking Your Seat
Guidelines for Receiving the Offering
Guidelines for Counting the Offering
Supplies Needed to Count the Offering

9 HANDLING THE COMMUNION SERVICE 86

Purchasing a Communion Set
Purchasing the Elements
Preparing the Elements
Setting the Table
General Guidelines
When to Have Communion
Who Serves Communion
Guidelines for Ushers During Communion
Guidelines for Person in Charge
Cleaning and Storing the Communion Set

10 GUIDELINES FOR MINISTERING SUPERNATURALLY 97

Flow With the Spirit
General Guidelines for Altar Calls
Guidelines for a Salvation Altar Call
Basic Guidelines for Healing Lines
Specific Instructions:
   During the Healing Lines
   For the Catcher
   For the Back-up Man

      For Those Helping People Up
      For the Feeders of the Lines
      For Physically Handicapped People
      For Disturbances in the Healing Line

11 POST-SERVICE RESPONSIBILITIES 116

FINAL COMMENT 121

APPENDIX 1—
    USHERS APPLICATION FORM 123

APPENDIX 2—
    HANDOUT—"CRYING BABIES" 126

Foreword

As masses of people come to the Lord in these last days, meeting facilities are becoming more and more inadequate. Buildings and churches holding 250 to 1,000 people are no longer large enough to handle the growing crowds. As a result, churches that teach the uncompromised Word of God, with signs and wonders following, are continually seeking larger meeting places so the needs of the people can be met.

Shopping centers and department stores that have gone out of business are frequent meeting places for God's people—as are theaters, concert halls, assembly centers, and outdoor sports fields.

Proverbs 13:22 says, *"The wealth of the sinner is laid up for the just."* God has enabled the secular world to use its knowledge and wealth to build large arenas and concert halls for satanic events. Now the time has come for these same arenas and large facilities to be used for God's work—for teaching God's Word!

It is vital—even in small services—that order and reverence for the Holy Spirit be maintained. However, it will become even more crucial as bodies of believers continue to grow in size.

The lack of teaching and training in maintaining order in services and in creating an atmosphere of reverence for the Holy Spirit has led me to write this handbook—USHERING IN HIS EXCELLENCE—for the ministry of helps today.

Although the ushers team is only one facet of the ministry of helps, this is God's calling upon my life. The talents, skills, and abilities with which the

Lord has equipped me are strongest in this area of service.

The Lord ministered to me several years ago in a dynamic way, showing me that the ministry of helps—and particularly a unified ushers team—would become known around the world for its work in setting an atmosphere for services, allowing the supernatural power of God to flow freely, giving the Holy Spirit TOTAL FREEDOM for having His way in every service.

Thus, the primary purpose for writing this handbook is to bring about unity in the ushers team . . . to equip them to assist not only the minister, but the entire congregation in functioning with order, harmony, love, and reverence toward the Holy Spirit.

The usher is no longer just a "bucket passer." His duties are much more diversified. Ushering is a ministry ordained by the Lord Jesus Christ. Ushers stand in the same ranks as Stephen, Philip, and the disciples—called to an area of "helps," but anointed to preach and teach the Word of God with signs and wonders following.

This handbook defines the ministry of helps, the purposes and functions of an ushers team, preparations for services, handling various challenges during services, how to flow with the one ministering, and how to close the services properly.

May you USHER IN HIS EXCELLENCE as you apply the principles presented in this handbook!

1
What Is The "Ministry Of Helps"

The ministry of helps is listed by Paul with the other ministry gifts in 1 Corinthians 12:28—*"And God hath set some in the church, first apostles, secondarily prophets, thirdly teachers, after that miracles, then gifts of healings, HELPS, governments, diversities of tongues."*

People called to the ministry of helps basically have the same burden and vision for sharing the Good News of the Lord Jesus Christ as the minister or speaker.

They include a great variety of people behind the scenes—maintenance personnel, sound men, secretaries, administrative personnel, counselors, bookkeepers, greeters, ushers, nursery workers, the advisory board, and others.

The ministry of helps will play a vital role in these last days because as the meetings become larger, it will be impossible for one person—the pastor or speaker—to make all of the arrangements. It's sad to say, but many pastors today are still responsible for mowing the grass, dusting and cleaning the facilities, setting up chairs, turning on the lights, getting the doors unlocked, adjusting the sound system, picking up paper, emptying the trash, operating as a business manager as well as doing all of the bookkeeping work.

The pastor needs to be freed of all these duties, so he can spend time in prayer and in the Word, preparing for his main duty—ministering the Word of God to the people.

If the pastor is free to function in this capacity, without becoming bogged down with the other technical cares of the church's function, he will be a beautiful channel through whom the Holy Spirit can do His work in this last hour.

For this to happen, the pastor needs men and women serving in the area of "helps" who will flow with the supernatural anointing of God, who will be sensitive to the Spirit of God, who will all be speaking the same thing, and who will be walking in unity and love toward one another—and toward the Body of Christ as well.

Most churches and church members fail to recognize that the ministry of helps is a "ministry." Some members still look upon ushers as "bucket passers," but when the team is properly developed, the person ministering can be assured of three things:

1. There will be order in the service.

2. The Holy Spirit will have freedom in the service to perfect His work.

3. There will be reverence toward the work of the Holy Spirit.

When these things are assured, the Body of Christ will be able to move into new realms of ministry, where the gifts of the Spirit and the supernatural power of God will flow as never before.

The Disciples in the "Helps" Ministry

The disciples were involved in a "helps" ministry as they accompanied Jesus in His ministry.

"And it came to pass afterward, that he (Jesus) went throughout every city and village, preaching and shewing the glad tidings of the kingdom of God: and the twelve were with him" (Luke 8:1).

The disciples served in whatever capacity was needed. They instantly obeyed in doing what Jesus asked them to do. We get a clearer picture of this in the scriptural account of the feeding of the five thousand.

"And Jesus, when he came out, saw much people, and was moved with compassion toward them, because they were as sheep not having a shepherd: and he began to teach them many things. And when the day was now far spent, his disciples came unto him, and said, This is a desert place, and now the time is far passed: Send them away, that they may go into the country round about, and into the villages, and buy themselves bread: for they have nothing to eat.

"He answered and said unto them, Give ye them to eat. And they say unto him, Shall we go and buy two hundred pennyworth of bread, and give them to eat? He saith unto them, How many loaves have ye? go and see. And when they knew, they say, Five, and two fishes. And he commanded them to make all sit down by companies upon the green grass. And they sat down in ranks, by hundreds, and by fifties.

"And when he had taken the five loaves and the two fishes, he looked up to heaven, and blessed, and

brake the loaves, and gave them to his disciples to set before them; and the two fishes divided he among them all. And they did all eat, and were filled. And they took up twelve baskets full of the fragments, and of the fishes" (Mark 6:34-43).

The disciples were a vital part of the feeding of the five thousand as they functioned in the "helps" ministry—ORGANIZING the masses of people and GUIDING them where to sit, FEEDING the multitude as Jesus directed, and PICKING up the leftovers.

The disciples also served in the ministry of helps as they assisted Jesus in the healing of blind Bartimaeus.

"And they came to Jericho: and as he went out of Jericho with his disciples and a great number of people, blind Bartimaeus, the son of Timaeus, sat by the highway side begging. And when he heard that it was Jesus of Nazareth, he began to cry out, and say, Jesus, thou son of David, have mercy on me. And many charged him that he should hold his peace: but he cried the more a great deal, Thou son of David, have mercy on me.

"And Jesus stood still, and commanded him to be called. And they call the blind man, saying unto him, Be of good comfort, rise; he calleth thee" (Mark 10:46-49).

In each of these scriptural accounts, you can see that the disciples were an extension of the arms of Jesus.

The disciples walked in the capacity of the ministry of helps again as they went to get the colt for Jesus for His triumphant entry into Jerusalem.

"And when they drew nigh unto Jerusalem, and were come to Bethphage, unto the mount of Olives, then sent Jesus two disciples, saying unto them, Go into the village over against you, and straightway ye shall find an ass tied, and a colt with her: loose them, and bring them unto me. And if any man say aught unto you, ye shall say, The Lord hath need of them; and straightway he will send them.

"All this was done, that it might be fulfilled which was spoken by the prophet, saying, Tell ye the daughter of Sion, Behold, thy King cometh unto thee, meek, and sitting upon an ass, and a colt the foal of an ass. And the disciples went, and did as Jesus commanded them" (Matthew 21:1-6).

If Jesus needed the assistance and help of the disciples, isn't it quite feasible that pastors and speakers today need to follow His example?

Jesus held fast to the specific things to which He was called, having the disciples perform many duties that simply complemented and strengthened what He did. He was constantly about the Father's business.

Pastors and speakers today must also be totally free to do one thing—to be about the Father's business! When this becomes so, with the ministry of helps performing its duties in an excellent manner, the Body of Christ will immediately step into a new realm of ministry with the gifts of the Spirit fluently operating, healings occurring en masse, as the Word is spoken with power, authority, and might.

When the pastor or speaker becomes bogged down with the cares of this life—with the nitty-gritty details of the ministry—his work is hindered, the work of the Holy Spirit is bound, and he is unable to fulfill the call that God has placed upon his life.

As we examine one more scriptural account of the ministry of helps operating in the ministry of Jesus, we begin to get a clearer picture of its function.

"And he sendeth forth two of his disciples, and saith unto them, Go ye into the city, and there shall meet you a man bearing a pitcher of water: follow him. And wheresoever he shall go in, say ye to the goodman of the house, The Master saith, Where is the guestchamber, where I shall eat the passover with my disciples?

"And he will shew you a large upper room furnished and prepared: there make ready for us. And his disciples went forth, and came into the city, and found as he had said unto them: and they made ready the passover" (Mark 14:13-16).

What an honor to work alongside of Jesus. What an honor to prepare the passover for Him!

Whether you realize it or not, that is your duty today as part of a unified, effective ushers team—**YOU BECOME AN EXTENSION OF THE ARMS OF JESUS** as you assist His chosen ones in their respective ministries.

And when you become an extension of Jesus' arms, people will be ministered to effectively, healings will take place en masse, sinners will be drawn by the supernatural power of God that so fluently prevails in every service.

And because you are developing excellency in being that extended arm of Jesus, many will be added to the Kingdom of God in this last hour before the trumpet sounds . . . all because of YOUR CONTRIBUTION to the ministry of helps!

2
Why Ushers?

An usher fulfills the role of a "helper" or "minister" to the pastor or speaker and to the congregation serving as unto the Lord.

He is a minister, called of God with a vision and a burden for the ministry, and equipped with the skills, talents, wisdom, and knowledge to carry out the calling which God has placed upon his life. This is no little task! An effective usher truly becomes "a servant of all."

"But so shall it not be among you: but whosoever will be great among you, shall be your minister: And whosoever of you will be the chiefest, shall be servant of all. For even the Son of man came not to be ministered unto, but to minister and to give his life a ransom for many" (Mark 10:43-45).

A united ushers team sets an atmosphere so charged with reverence and sensitivity that the Spirit of God can have His perfect way in EVERY service. This results in giant steps being taken into the spiritual realm.

In these last days, masses of people are coming into the Kingdom of God; and the church is drawing the sinner because of the supernatural that is openly taking place. As the sinner is convicted and baby Christians fill the churches, the need to maintain order, reverence, and respect for the Holy Spirit is greater than ever before.

Therefore, the ushers team must come together in complete harmony, unity, love, and excellence as never before to keep pace with God's ongoing work.

Responsibilities of the Head Usher

An ushers team that walks in excellence is headed by an usher that has a complete vision of the purpose and function of his team. He knows what a unified team can do to enhance the work of God. His goal is to develop and perfect just such a team. This person is called the "head usher."

An effective head usher builds up his team. He lets them know they are "God's best" and encourages them to perform in such a manner. He guides them in how to dress appropriately for their role.

The ushers team is not a one-man show! One person cannot do the entire job. It must be a team effort to be a successful ministry. Each usher must speak and do the same thing in each service, being joined together in the same mind, in one accord, united in faith and utterance. This can only happen as the head usher assumes his responsibilities, some of which include:

1. Delegating responsibilities to team members.

2. Teaching and training each usher for his respective assignments.

3. Teaching ushers to think on their own.

4. Ensuring that the pastor or speaker will be able to minister at his best without disturbances.

5. Being alert to the needs of the one ministering prior to the service, during the service, and following the service.

6. Serving in a public relations position.

7. Assisting the total ushering team in helping people find their seats.

8. Heading the control of movement during the service.

9. Directing the receiving of offerings, particularly for security purposes.

10. Assisting directly in the communion services.

11. Flowing inconspicuously with the laying-on-of-hands ministry.

12. Helping with the altar calls.

13. Supervising his team in handling disturbances involving crying babies, small children, out-of-order adults, and seating people.

14. Ensuring that every person who comes to the meeting will receive what he or she needs from the Lord before leaving the service. (With the help of his effective team, this will be done.)

15. Training the ushers team to take over during his absence.

The head usher needs to be in a position to help expand the vision of his ushering team; to make them aware of the calling God has placed on their lives; to teach and train ushers and volunteer workers so they will enhance the fulfillment of the vision God has given the Body of Christ.

Once the ushers team has been selected, the head usher will need to set up weekly training sessions to bring the ushers into a complete team, equipped to walk and talk in one accord.

3

What To Look For In An Usher

Let's examine the Scriptures to see what personal qualities were important in the people named to leadership positions in the ministry of Jesus. These same qualities are needed in the leadership that becomes a part of the ministry of helps today. The first scriptural account is the choosing of the seven deacons.

Choosing of the Seven Deacons

"And in those days, when the number of the disciples was multiplied, there arose a murmuring of the Grecians against the Hebrews, because their widows were neglected in the daily ministration. Then the twelve called the multitude of the disciples unto them, and said, It is not reason that we should leave the word of God, and serve tables. Wherefore, brethren, look ye out among you seven men of honest report, full of the Holy Ghost and wisdom, whom we may appoint over this business. But we will give ourselves continually to prayer, and to the ministry of the word.

"And the saying pleased the whole multitude: and they chose Stephen, a man full of faith and of the Holy Ghost, and Philip, and Prochorus, and Nicanor, and Timon, and Parmenas, and Nicolas a

proselyte of Antioch: Whom they set before the apostles: and when they had prayed, they laid their hands on them. And the word of God increased; and the number of the disciples multiplied in Jerusalem greatly; and a great company of the priests were obedient to the faith. And Stephen, full of faith and power, did great wonders and miracles among the people" (Acts 6:1-8).

Some of the qualities for leadership in this passage of Scripture include:

1. Being of a GOOD REPUTATION or OF AN HONEST REPORT (men of integrity).

2. Being FULL OF THE HOLY GHOST. (They were all filled with the Holy Ghost and spoke with other tongues—Acts 2:4.)

3. Being FULL OF WISDOM. (Practical wisdom to run the business aspect of their ministry and the wisdom of God to minister the Word of God.)

4. Being full of FAITH and POWER.

The Scripture verses examined in this chapter reveal other qualities that an usher who desires to walk in excellence must develop. Set these qualities as "goals for growth."

You Must Have a Single Eye

To walk with a single eye is to walk with your body, soul, and spirit filled to overflowing with the life of God. You can overflow with the life of God as you fill your mind with the Word of God, meditate upon His Word, and maintain a goal of DESIRING

TO PLEASE THE HEAVENLY FATHER WITH ALL THAT YOU SAY AND DO—EVERY MINUTE OF EVERY DAY.

"The light of the body is the eye: if therefore thine eye be single, thy whole body shall be full of light" (Matthew 6:22).

You Must Work as Unto the Lord

Your work as an usher must be "as unto the Lord." If you are working to please the head usher or other people before your desire to please the Father, you will never find satisfaction in what you do.

"And whatsoever ye do in word or deed, do all in the name of the Lord Jesus, giving thanks to God and the Father by him. And whatsoever ye do, do it heartily, as to the Lord, and not unto men" (Colossians 3:17, 23).

You Must Be Filled with the Word of God

In the following verses, you will see that the Word of God is your "life" and your "health." You cannot develop to a point of excellence in ushering without God's life and God's health. They are yours if you simply take time daily to "feed on the Word of God."

"My son, attend to my words; incline thine ear unto my sayings. Let them not depart from thine eyes; keep them in the midst of thine heart. For they are life unto those that find them, and health to all their flesh" (Proverbs 4:20-22).

You Must Be Strong in Faith

How do you become strong in faith?

"So then faith cometh by hearing, and hearing by the word of God" (Romans 10:17).

Faith comes as you spend time studying and meditating upon the Word of God, allowing the Word to take root in your spirit—not just in your head! Take time daily in the Word and in fellowship with the Father to develop your life of faith. The Word also says that *"the just shall live by faith"* (Romans 1:17b).

As you grow in faith, you will learn to call those things forth that be not as though they were—even in the performance of your total ushers team!

"Who . . . calleth those things which be not as though they were" (Romans 4:17).

You Must Be Led by the Spirit of God

Be sensitive to the leading of the Holy Spirit. You will develop your sensitivity as you spend time with the Father, spend time in the Word, spend time in prayer, and spend time in quietness before Him.

"For as many as are led by the Spirit of God, they are the sons of God" (Romans 8:14).

You Must Be a Person Who Speaks "Faith-filled" Words

What you say turns the events of your personal life around, and it also has a direct effect on the unity and excellence of the total ushers team. Be a person of words that are faith-filled, edifying, and loving—for you receive what you SAY.

"For verily I say unto you, That whosoever shall SAY unto this mountain, Be thou removed, and be thou cast into the sea; and shall not doubt in his heart, but shall believe that those things which he SAITH shall come to pass; he shall have whatsoever he SAITH. Therefore I say unto you, What things soever ye desire, when ye pray, believe that ye receive them, and ye shall have them" (Mark 11:23, 24).

You Must Control Your Tongue

As a member of the ushers team, you will have many excellent opportunities to say things with your tongue that should not be said. You CAN control your tongue with the help of the Holy Spirit.

"For in many things we offend all, if any man offend not in word, the same is a perfect man, and able also to bridle the whole body. Behold, we put bits in the horses' mouths, that they may obey us; and we turn about their whole body. Behold also the ships, which though they be so great, and are driven of fierce winds, yet are they turned about with a very small helm, whithersoever the governor listeth.

"Even so the tongue is a little member, and boasteth great things. Behold, how great a matter a little fire kindleth! And the tongue is a fire, a world of iniquity: so is the tongue among our members, that it defileth the whole body, and setteth on fire the course of nature; and it is set on fire of hell. For

every kind of beasts, and of birds, and of serpents, and of things in the sea, is tamed, and hath been tamed of mankind: But the tongue can no man tame; it is an unruly evil, full of deadly poison" (James 3: 2-8).

As you learn to let the Holy Spirit dominate your tongue, you will be heading toward the goal of a "perfect man."

You are cautioned in the Word of God to "bridle" your tongue. A bridle is used for RESTRAINT.

"If any man among you seem to be religious, and bridleth not his tongue, but deceiveth his own heart, this man's religion is vain" (James 1: 26).

Again in the following passage of Scripture, you see the importance of choosing wisely the words that you speak.

"Let no corrupt communication proceed out of your mouth, but that which is good to the use of edifying, that it may minister grace unto the hearers. And grieve not the holy Spirit of God, whereby ye are sealed unto the day of redemption.

"Let all bitterness, and wrath, and anger, and clamour, and evil speaking, be put away from you, with all malice: And be ye kind one to another, tenderhearted, forgiving one another, even as God for Christ's sake hath forgiven you" (Ephesians 4: 29-32).

You Must Be Free of Backbiting

Backbiting does not contribute to a life of holiness; rather, it can become like a rampant disease.

The following Scripture verses say that backbiting even keeps you from abiding in the tabernacle of the Lord. And no one can afford to be barred from the presence of the Lord!

"Lord, who shall abide in thy tabernacle? who shall dwell in thy holy hill? He that walketh uprightly, and worketh righteousness, and speaketh the truth in his heart. He that backbiteth not with his tongue, nor doeth evil to his neighbour, nor taketh up a reproach against his neighbour" (Psalm 15:1-3).

If an usher (or one of your brothers) offends you, resort to prayer—not to backbiting! Backbiting will only hinder your own walk with the Lord by blocking your communication channel with Him.

You Must Be Filled with the Compassion of Jesus

Your compassion will develop as you come into a life of adoration of the Lord Jesus Christ and of the heavenly Father. His compassion will enable you to feel what others feel and to hurt when others hurt, for one purpose—to set the captives free!

Over and over in the ministry of Jesus, the Word of God says that "He was moved with compassion." That must also be your motive—to touch others with the compassion of Jesus that they might be set free.

"But when he (Jesus) saw the multitudes, he was moved with compassion on them, because they fainted, and were scattered abroad, as sheep having no shepherd" (Matthew 9:36).

You Must Walk in Obedience

No matter what your age, you will never outgrow the need to walk in total obedience to God and to those in authority over you.

"But this thing commanded I them, saying, Obey my voice, and I will be your God, and ye shall be my people: and walk ye in all the ways that I have commanded you, that it may be well unto you" (Jeremiah 7:23).

God's Word commands us to be "willing" and "obedient."

"If ye be willing and obedient, ye shall eat the good of the land: But if ye refuse and rebel, ye shall be devoured with the sword: for the mouth of the Lord hath spoken it" (Isaiah 1:19, 20).

As an usher, you must first walk in obedience to the Lord.

Second, you must walk in obedience to the authority placed over you—the head usher. With these priorities correct, you can do more to create unity and harmony in the ushers team by having a willingness to please the head usher, the man God has placed in authority over you. This sets the pace and atmosphere for USHERING IN HIS EXCELLENCE!

"Servants, obey in all things your masters according to the flesh; not with eye service, as menpleasers; but in singleness of heart, fearing God" (Colossians 3:22).

You Must Walk in the "Power" of God

You need to walk in the power of God with which He has equipped you.

"Behold, I give unto you power to tread on serpents and scorpions, and over all the power of the enemy: and nothing shall by any means hurt you" (Luke 10:19).

You Must Walk in the "Might" of God

To be effective in your ministry as an usher, you must walk in the "might" of God. Pray this passage of Scripture over yourself and over the total ushers team DAILY.

"For this cause I bow my knees unto the Father of our Lord Jesus Christ, of whom the whole family in heaven and earth is named, that he would grant you, according to the riches of his glory, to be strengthened with might by his Spirit in the inner man; that Christ may dwell in your hearts by faith; that ye, being rooted and grounded in love, may be able to comprehend with all saints what is the breadth, and length, and depth, and height; and to know the love of Christ, which passeth knowledge, that ye might be filled with all the fulness of God" (Ephesians 3:14-19).

You Must Be Faithful

It is so important to be faithful. It is through faithfulness that the hand of the Father exalts His children.

"He that is faithful in that which is least is faithful also in much: and he that is unjust in the least is unjust also in much" (Luke 16:10).

Learn to be faithful in the little things, in the little tasks, in the unpleasant tasks . . . for God promotes His children only when they become faithful in the little things which they have been called to do.

You Must Always Be Dependable

Faithfulness and dependability go hand in hand. The qualities that you develop in your personal life carry over into your ministry. Always be dependable. If you say you will do something, keep your word.

"But whoso keepeth his word, in him verily is the love of God perfected: hereby know we that we are in him. He that saith he abideth in him ought himself also so to walk, even as he walked" (1 John 2:5, 6).

When you are asked to do something, always follow through with that task to completion!

You Must Prefer Others Above Yourself

Learn to think of God first, others second, and then yourself.

"Be kindly affectioned one to another with brotherly love; in honour preferring one another" (Romans 12:10).

If you truly prefer someone, you will love him with a Christ-like love.

"Thou shalt love thy neighbour as thyself. Love worketh no ill to his neighbour: therefore love is the fulfilling of the law" (Romans 13:9, 10).

You Must Be Free of Envy and Strife

Allow no place for envy and strife in your personal life nor in your work with the ushers team. The Word says that envy is as rottenness to your bones! Strife falls into the same category.

"A sound heart is the life of the flesh: but envy the rottenness of the bones" (Proverbs 14:30).

You Must Rejoice Over Others' Blessings

Learn to rejoice over your brother's blessings, honors, or special recognitions. As you learn to rejoice with your brother, blessings will come your way.

"Rejoice with them that do rejoice, and weep with them that weep" (Romans 12:15).

You Must Walk in Instant Forgiveness

You will have many opportunities in your ministry as an usher to walk in forgiveness. Don't let it become a challenge to forgive those that offend you.

Rather, let it be a privilege to keep your spirit man so quickened with the Word that you will find it joyous to walk in instant forgiveness toward all men.

"For if ye forgive men their trespasses, your heavenly Father will also forgive you: but if ye forgive not men their trespasses, neither will your Father forgive your trespasses" (Matthew 6:14, 15).

Another passage of Scripture puts it this way:

"Judge not, and ye shall not be judged: condemn not, and ye shall not be condemned: forgive, and ye shall be forgiven. Give, and it shall be given unto

you; good measure, pressed down, and shaken together, and running over, shall men give into your bosom. For with the same measure that ye mete withal it shall be measured to you again" (Luke 6:37, 38).

Many times these verses are limited to "financial" giving in our thinking and application. However, this same kind of giving in other areas will come back to you in like measure, in like kind, as spoken forth in the Word—in giving FORGIVENESS, LOVE, COMPASSION, GENTLENESS, WISDOM, KNOWLEDGE, UNDERSTANDING, TIME, SKILLS, and TALENTS.

You Must Be a Doer of the Word

Your ministry as an usher involves "doing the Word" and not just hearing it. You have multitudes of opportunities at every service to be a doer of the Word of God.

"But be ye doers of the word, and not hearers only, deceiving your own selves. For if any be a hearer of the word, and not a doer, he is like unto a man beholding his natural face in a glass: For he beholdeth himself, and goeth his way, and straightway forgetteth what manner of man he was. But whoso looketh into the perfect law of liberty, and continueth therein, he being not a forgetful hearer, but a doer of the work, this man shall be blessed in his deed" (James 1:22-25).

You Must Be an Intercessor

You can break down Satan's barriers in your own life through intercession. Likewise, as you join the ushers team in group intercession before every service, you will be able to break down Satan's work before it has a chance to start. You are called to intercession for your country's leaders and for all who are in authority.

"I exhort therefore, that, first of all, supplications, prayers, intercessions, and giving of thanks, be made for all men; for kings, and for all that are in authority; that we may lead a quiet and peaceable life in all godliness and honesty. For this is good and acceptable in the sight of God our Saviour; who will have all men to be saved, and to come unto the knowledge of the truth" (1 Timothy 2:1-4).

God commands us to pray in our spirit as well as with our understanding.

"I will pray with the spirit, and I will pray with the understanding also: I will sing with the spirit, and I will sing with the understanding also" (1 Corinthians 14:15).

Here's another passage of Scripture that reinforces the importance of intercession:

"Likewise the Spirit also helpeth our infirmities: for we know not what we should pray for as we ought: but the Spirit itself maketh intercession for us with groanings which cannot be uttered. And he that searcheth the hearts knoweth what is the mind of the Spirit, because he maketh intercession for the saints according to the will of God" (Romans 8:26, 27).

With proper preparation before every service, which includes intercessory prayer, you have put every person that comes to a service in a position to receive from God! Hallelujah!

You Must Always Keep Yourself Built Up In the Spirit

It is very easy to respond to negative circumstances, situations, and criticisms in a negative (or wrong) way if you are not built up in the Spirit. And such opportunities are plenteous in your ministry as an usher! But if you are built up in your spirit, you will ALWAYS respond in love. How do you build up your spirit man—the real you—by praying every day in the Holy Ghost.

"But ye, beloved, building up yourselves on your most holy faith, praying in the Holy Ghost, keep yourselves in the love of God, looking for the mercy of our Lord Jesus Christ unto eternal life" (Jude 20, 21).

As you strive to develop each of the qualities mentioned in this chapter and any others in the Word of God which have not been covered here, you will truly USHER IN HIS EXCELLENCE!

4
Why Hold Ushers Meetings?

The head usher needs to schedule regular training sessions for his ushers team, preferably on a weekly basis. This enhances each usher's ability to walk in unity, harmony, and in one accord, which, in turn, sets the pace for God to do a mighty work in EVERY service.

Applications—Before the First Meeting

Every potential usher needs to fill out an application form, available from the head usher. (Sample application form is given in Appendix 1, pages 124-125.)

It is then the responsibility of the head usher to screen the applications, set up individual interviews should he feel the need, and then make selections for his team.

All of the ushers, once selected, need to come in line with the authority that God has invested in the head usher. This is a "must" for the ushers to operate as a unified team.

The Ushers Meetings

These guidelines need to be followed for meaningful ushers meetings:

1. It is the head usher's responsibility (unless he delegates this duty to another person) to make the contacts with his ushers team to let them know about their training meetings. (This may be done by letter or by telephone.)

2. The meetings must be at a regularly scheduled DAY and TIME to ensure consistency of attendance.

3. All of the ushers need to attend every meeting. Otherwise, it puts an additional burden upon the head usher, as he must hold extra training sessions to bring these members up to date on training information.

4. The meetings need to be structured to provide one basic teaching at each meeting.

5. The meetings need to give the ushers an opportunity to openly communicate with the head usher, particularly in the following areas:

a. Any possible problem areas.

b. Any suggestions for improvement on any aspect of ushering.

c. Any general comments that would enhance the efficiency and excellency of the team.

6. The meetings need to provide time to join in intercessory prayer for one another and for the services.

The Importance of "Oneness"

In organizing the ushers team and scheduling training sessions, you need to remember that God gave the Spirit WITHOUT MEASURE to the Lord Jesus Christ. He did not give the Spirit without measure to any man; therefore, each man has a "portion" of the Spirit.

As you join in "oneness" in your ushers team, coming together in one accord, with one goal, joining the skills, talents, wisdom, knowledge, power, and might of God invested in each usher—you become much stronger toward the quality of "the Spirit without measure" which Jesus had.

You cannot afford to have your ushers each doing his own thing. The more united the ushers team, the more excellency will result in every service, for then the Holy Spirit can have His way and the Spirit of God at work in your services will cause a mighty outpouring of the work of the Holy Spirit!

5

Pre-Service Responsibilities

Once the head usher is named, and he has selected his team and begun to train them, there are many practical things that need to be done before people begin to arrive for a service.

The responsibility for everything to run smoothly during a service falls back on the head usher. Therefore, he must:

- Learn to delegate authority.

- Teach his team to work smart, not hard.

- Learn to follow up on the individual ushers to be sure their tasks are completed.

You will find discussed in this chapter many of the technical areas of responsibility that need to be taken care of before the doors open for a service. An atmosphere must be created that is not only conducive to excellency in ushering, but which gives the Holy Spirit FULL REIGN in the service.

Ushers Team Needs to Arrive Early

The head usher and his team need to arrive at least one hour before the service is to start. This will give them sufficient time to take care of any maintenance duties that have been neglected or to take care of any other inconsistencies.

This will also give the ushers team an opportunity to pray and bind Satan over the service and to loose the Holy Spirit to have His perfect way in the service.

The ushers team has a tremendous responsibility in setting the atmosphere for the entire service.

Uniform Dress Code for Ushers

Ushers need to follow a dress code, wearing matching sports jackets if possible. This will enable you to be readily identifiable by members of the congregation and by members of the speaker's team should they have questions.

The ushers team needs to be extremely neat in appearance, with all members of the team dressed uniformly. That is, in addition to the matching jackets, if it is possible, you need to wear:

- White shirts.

- Black shoes.

- Black pants

- Black ties.

Identify the Ushers Room

If the ushers have a special "Ushers Room," you need to be aware of it so you can dress and/or prepare for the service in that room. This room is also usually used for the storage of the ushers' materials for each service.

Materials and Supplies Needed for Ushers Room

The ushers will need to have a sufficient quantity of materials and supplies on hand for use in each service.

Materials needed will include:

1. Offering envelopes.
2. Visitation cards or packets.
3. Speaker's handouts, if any.
4. Special envelopes or cards, if any.
5. If there are envelope jackets on the chairs, be sure the supply is replenished for each service.

Supplies needed will include:

1. Paper or posterboard (or cardboard) to make signs at the last minute, if needed.
2. Masking tape.
3. Magic markers.
4. Straight pins.
5. Extra pencils and pens.

Transportation for Speaker

The head usher should know who is responsible for the transportation of the one ministering. Most churches will furnish a car for the speaker to use, and some will even furnish a driver for him.

Whether the speaker has his own car or is using one from the church, the car should be parked as close to the exit door as possible. This is good in case of adverse weather conditions; it is also important if the one ministering has been under a strong anointing, for when this happens, he will many times not only need help to get to his car, but he will need someone to drive him to his destination as well.

The head usher, or the person to whom he has delegated this responsibility, will remain alert to this situation should it arise.

The Speaker's Room

The speaker's room, sometimes called the prophet's chamber, is a room set aside where the one ministering can be alone with God—to spend time in the Word, in prayer, and in quietness before the Lord.

This special room is also a place where he can talk with friends or other ministers without being disturbed. It should be a place where he can prepare himself before he steps onto the platform (such as combing his hair, checking his tie, using the restroom, or even getting a bite to eat or drink).

Some of the supplies that should be provided in the speaker's room include:

1. A restroom.

2. A small kitchen, furnished with dishes, silverware, pots and pans.

3. A small stove or microwave.

4. A refrigerator.

5. Coffee pot for coffee or hot water for tea.

6. Juice, water, milk.

7. Snacks, such as crackers, cookies, cheese, peanut butter, bread, jelly, nuts, something sweet—mints, chewing gum, breath spray, etc.

8. Sugar and cream, lemons and honey, for coffee or tea.

9. Napkins.

10. Meats and spreads for sandwiches.

11. A coat room.

12. A small reading area with desk.

13. A place to rest, such as easy chairs or a couch, a place to eat, such as a small dining room table with chairs.

14. A telephone.

15. The room should be wired for sound so the speaker can hear what is going on in the service if it has already begun. The sound should have a switch to control it should it get too loud.

16. Good lighting, heat, and air-conditioning.

17. Paper and pencils.

You need to treat the one ministering with the same kindness and attention that you would give to Jesus.

Security for the Speaker's Room

It is common courtesy for an usher to be at the exit door of the speaker's room to assist the speaker to the platform as he leaves the room. This person would also be responsible for keeping the public from entering this area. The door should have a lock on it.

An usher should also be waiting at the door of the auditorium. This usher must be a strong person, who is motivated by courtesy and love, as it will be his responsibility to discourage people from entering the speaker's room.

If people insist on seeing the speaker or talking with him personally, this same usher should have them write their message on a piece of paper so they won't be completely turned away, and yet so the minister is free to obey the Spirit of the Lord without disturbances.

Handling the Speaker's Messages

There are special guidelines that will help you handle the speaker's messages, for he will receive all types of notes, letters, and messages.

1. First, ALL messages and notes for the speaker should be given to the head usher. The head usher is the only one that will contact the speaker, unless this responsibility has been delegated to another usher.

2. When the speaker arrives, the head usher should talk with him to see if he wants his mail or if he wants the head usher to screen it first.

a. Most speakers want only messages that are edifying and uplifting, particularly before a service. They do not want to receive letters before the service that are upsetting or negative, for this type of letter will serve as an effort to draw their attention from the things of God.

b. Many of the notes deal with disagreement with the speaker on a certain topic he discussed, while others are words of thanks, words of testimony, notes from personal friends, or notes from a large contributor to his ministry.

c. Other notes deal with requests for special prayer, those seeking a word from the Lord through the speaker, or people wanting to tell the speaker their life story so he will be able to tell them the will of God for their lives.

 1) In most cases, if people will listen to the speaker as he ministers, he will answer their questions.

 2) If you and the counselors both still feel the need for the person to speak with the one ministering, the speaker should be consulted. It is then his decision whether or not he will speak with the person making the request.

3. Sometimes it is best to screen the speaker's mail, give him only emergency items, and hold the remaining mail until he concludes his seminar or speaking engagement. Obey the instructions of the one ministering.

Be Alert to the Speaker's Needs

You should make every effort to meet the needs of the speaker. Try to find out in advance some of the following details:

1. Does the speaker desire carpet on the floor for the healing lines?

2. Does the speaker prefer a wireless mike?

3. Is there a way for the speaker to leave the platform and come into the congregation if he prefers?

You will easily learn to discern what the speaker wants by the tone of his voice and/or his gestures. However, if you know in advance how the speaker usually handles the altar calls for salvation, for the baptism in the Holy Spirit, and for healings, this will help you a great deal.

Handling of Announcements

Any announcements to be taken to the platform will usually be handled by only one person—the head usher. The following guidelines should be followed when handling announcements:

1. All announcements should be typed neatly and be well-worded.

2. Be sure that all of the announcements are complete (containing why's, when's, if's, and but's, etc.)

3. If there is an announcement involving the death of a person, it should be taken to the platform as quickly as possible without dis-

turbing the one ministering or the congregation. (Otherwise, give it to the person in charge of the meeting, and he will follow through with it.)

4. Announcements concerning car lights that have been left on need to be taken to the platform and announced BEFORE the service begins. (Do NOT interrupt the flow of the service once it has begun. If the announcement cannot be made, simply stand by with jumper cables to assist once the service is over.)

5. The podium is to be used only by the person or persons in charge of teaching and preaching. It is not for fellowship and/or transferring messages like a telephone!

Arranging the Platform

Only one usher should be assigned the responsibility of setting up the platform properly. Some of the guidelines that will help this usher include:

1. Be sure ice water is brought to the podium for the speaker.

2. Be sure that the microphone wires are out of the way and functioning.

3. One usher needs to be assigned to be the speaker's "runner" should he need anything.

4. Only those people who have been authorized should be on the platform. (This gives a much more organized appearance.)

Arranging the Seating for Services

The seating for each service needs to be arranged before anyone is allowed in the building for the service. It should be arranged according to the preference of the one ministering.

If the service is to be held in a regular auditorium, most of the seats are secured to the floor. However, there may be the need to set up folding chairs in specified areas.

In nearly every service, whether large or small, you will need to reserve sections for the following people:

1. Blind section.

2. Deaf section.

3. Wheelchair section.

4. Cot section.

5. Special guests section.

6. Staff section.

7. Counselor's section.

8. Foreign visitor's section.

The reserved areas need to be clearly marked before anyone is allowed to come into the service. The seating of the total congregation will be completed in an orderly manner if this guideline is followed.

Special Seating Sections—Reserve Seating

One of the most difficult jobs for an usher is explaining why seats are being saved or reserved. Many times during large meetings, special sections of seats are reserved for the staff, friends of the ministry, for the deaf, foreign dignitaries, etc. When people come early to a meeting and the best seats in the house are already taken, they often are quite upset. Many will quote the Scriptures, and some will even write letters telling you that God is no respecter of persons. A favorite passage is James 2:2-4.

"For if there come unto your assembly a man with a gold ring, in goodly apparel, and there come in also a poor man in vile raiment; And ye have respect to him that weareth the gay clothing, and say unto him, Sit thou here in a good place; and say to the poor, Stand thou there, or sit here under my footstool: Are ye not then partial in yourselves, and are become judges of evil thoughts?"

They are right—God is no respecter of persons. But in order to handle the situation properly, you need the cooperation of the platform and of the people in charge. Many times the platform will have special sections reserved but will ask people not to hold seats between services or for late arrivers. Sometimes the statement is made that any Bibles or personal belongings left on the seats between meetings will be removed before the next meeting. This thrills those who have arrived late, but at the same time, it upsets those who desire to reserve their seats while they run out to get a quick bite to eat.

If the people in charge on the platform are merely making a token gesture and do not really want the ushers to remove the Bibles or personal belongings, then those who heard the announcements tend to get upset because the ushers are not doing anything.

In cases like these, the usher cannot win for losing. He is right in the middle, but the Lord has provided a way out. It's found in 1 Peter 2:20.

"If, when ye do well, and suffer for it, ye take it patiently, this is acceptable with God."

As an usher, you are to help and assist under the ministry or under the minister. The Scriptures say that, first of all, you must speak with authority (Matthew 7:29, Mark 1:22). They also say you are a man under authority (Matthew 8:9, Luke 7:8). You are servants and subject to masters according to 1 Peter 2:18. Christians are subject to each other (1 Peter 5:5), and to rulers and governments (Romans 13:1-5, Titus 3:1).

The Word says every soul is subject to a higher power. Obey the leaders that are over you, but know you are equal to those around you. You are under those that are over you, but over those who are under you.

As leaders we are to lead people to Christ. We are to submit ourselves to the elders and to every ordinance of man and be in subjection unto the Father.

As a minister or as an usher, you are to be aware of the situation that is best for the whole and do all things without murmuring and complaining. As long as we are working for another ministry and assisting another ministry, that ministry is in charge. The Word says that we are to give honor where honor is due. If the ministry wants to hold reserved seating for special friends, as ushers we are to uphold that decision and carry out the things that are asked of us.

Our job is to do the best we can possibly do—and walk in love. Handle the situation with authority, but remain in love. If someone is upset with the decision that has been made, pray for him . . . that the peace of God will stay upon him, so he can be ministered to and enjoy the service.

Handling Prayer Cloths

Some people will bring prayer cloths for the one ministering to anoint so they can give them to a particular person for healing and/or deliverance. One person, preferably the head usher, should take the responsibility of handling all of the prayer cloths, unless he delegates this responsibility to another usher.

Carefully consider the following guidelines for the handling of the prayer cloths:

1. Give all handkerchiefs and prayer cloths to the usher who has been delegated this responsibility.

2. Be alert to the location of where the prayer cloths and handkerchiefs are to be taken.

3. Be sure that the prayer cloths are removed from paper, plastic bags, or other containers.

4. Allow the person bringing the cloths to attach a name to the prayer cloths (with a small piece of paper or masking tape), especially if the meeting is to be a large service.

5. Should there be notes, letters, or messages of any type attached to the prayer cloths, they should be removed by the usher responsible for this area and given to the head usher.

6. In large meetings, there may be a need for special tables to be set up for the prayer cloths, which will usually be located to one side of the platform.

Handling of Ministry Cloths for the Healing Line

Ministry cloths are normally used in the healing line to cover the women's legs when they are slain in the Spirit.

The head usher needs to be alert, knowing in advance of the service the person who will be assisting the one ministering in this area. Usually the speaker's wife will be responsible for handling this part of the ministry. If the person is single, however, the head usher is responsible for finding a person to assume this responsibility.

You should let this person know, prior to the service, the location of the ministry cloths so she will be ready to assist the one ministering when the healing service begins.

Everyone who falls under the power does not need to be draped with a cloth—only those whose clothes have become disarranged in a manner that might cause embarrassment. The Holy Spirit is a gentleman, and when people fall under the power, they usually do so in a very peaceful and orderly manner. However, if a cloth is needed, this action should not be so obvious that it takes away from the ministry of the Holy Spirit.

Handling of the Book Tables

The head usher should know in advance how many tables are needed for books (usually there is one for the ministry and one for the guest speaker). You will then need to know who is responsible for setting up the tables. Here are some additional details:

1. Be sure the tables are available and set up as needed.
2. Know who is responsible for handling the money boxes for each table.
3. Fix responsibility in advance as to who is to take the tables down after the service.
4. If the tables are to remain for additional services, usually covering cloths are available for the book tables. If this is true, the head usher will need to also double check on the security for the tables for the time that the services are not in session.

Handling of the Sound System, Televising, and Taping

Handling the sound system, the televising, and the taping are usually not in the ushers' area of responsibility. Other people are usually assigned to these areas. However, the head usher must be alert to each person responsible for these areas. Should there be a need to contact these people before the services, during the services, or after the services, these people will be readily identifiable.

These people are usually also responsible for handling their own supplies. If this is not the case, however, one person should be assigned to double check on the supplies needed before the service begins.

There may also be the need to assign the responsibility for handling the special lighting for the televising to one usher.

Additional Usher Assignments

Additional usher assignments that need to be made prior to each service include:

1. Who is assigned to security?

2. Who is assigned to the parking lot, if other than the security people?

3. Who is responsible for handling the heating and air-conditioning?

4. Who is responsible for handling the lights in the main auditorium and on the platform?

5. Who is responsible for having an umbrella at hand should one be needed to assist the speaker from his car into the service?

Ushers Must Be Alert to Locations Throughout the Building

Every usher should be thoroughly acquainted with the various locations throughout the building so he will be able to give directions to any member of the congregation should there be the need to do so. Some of these locations are:

1. Children's classes.
2. Nurseries.
3. Telephones.
4. Restrooms.
5. Water fountains.
6. Lost and found.
7. Location of mops, brooms, buckets, soap, towels, toilet paper, etc.

Identify Counselors and Prayer Room

All ushers need to know the following details in regard to the area of counseling for each service:

1. Who is the head counselor?
2. Who are the other members of the counseling staff?
3. Is there a counselor's prayer room? If so, where is it located?
4. Do chairs need to be set up in the prayer and counseling room?

Ushers Assignments to Specific Locations

The head usher is responsible for making assignments to the ushers staff for each service. It is his responsibility to give them the location of their assignments and any other details that will assist them in carrying out their respective duties.

Placement of the ushers might include the following areas:

1. Halls.
2. Children's room.
3. Parking lot.
4. Speaker's room.
5. Special seating section.
6. Deaf section.
7. Blind section.
8. Staff section.
9. Foreign section.
10. Counselor's section.
11. Security seating.
12. Prayer line workers section.
13. Greeters or Hostesses section.
14. Book Table workers section.
15. Wheelchair section.
16. Ushers in back of auditorium.
17. Special cases—cots, special chairs, etc.

Once the doors are open for a service, there is no time to discuss assignments, directives, etc. with the ushers team. For when the doors open, even though the ushers have been at work for an hour or more, the MINISTRY of the ushers team begins. Every usher serves in a public relations position, walking in love toward all, and with responsibility for his assigned section.

The plan for the service has been organized in detail. Now it's time to work that plan!

6
Welcoming And Directing

Once the doors open for a service, it is too late to make new plans or to give detailed instructions to the ushers. The usher's job has now begun! By this time, all instructions should have been given according to the plans that have been organized. It is time to work the plan that has been set forth for the particular service.

1. What time does the service start?
2. Where are the restrooms?
3. Is this seat reserved?

You may have your mind on the things you have been assigned to do, but these questions are important to the ones asking them. You must remember that you are in a public relations position as well as in a position of ministry. Therefore, you must:

1. Walk in love, and let the love of Jesus Christ radiate through you at all times.

2. Take time to smile and be friendly. Take people's hands and greet them (even if they have already been greeted at the door) because a TOUCH of love is important!

3. Answer their questions to the best of your ability. If you don't know the answer, don't be embarrassed to say you don't know. However, check on their questions and give them answers.

4. Look sharp! Have your coat buttoned, shoes shined, tie in position, fresh breath, etc.

5. Watch your actions! A hurried usher with a worried look does not minister peace. If you have the joy of the Lord, let your face know it! If you don't, stop for prayer before the service begins.

6. Watch your words! Minister love, faith, and hope. Let Philippians 4:8 govern your words and actions.

   "Finally, brethren, whatsoever things are true, whatsoever things are honest, whatsoever things are just, whatsoever things are pure, whatsoever things are lovely, whatsoever things are of good report; if there be any virtue, and if there be any praise, think on these things."

7. Remember that you are in charge, so walk with the authority that God has invested in you. The real challenge of an usher usually begins as he attempts to maintain authority and walk in love at the same time.

8. Remember to work as a team, for it's not a one-man show! Teamwork sets an atmosphere for a stronger anointing to flow in the service.

Your chief purpose as an usher is to see that everyone who comes to the service receives what he has come for from the Lord before he leaves. To do this, you must carry out an orderly system of enforcing certain rules and regulations.

You must be ready for last-minute changes, but don't let changes upset you. Be flexible. Be able to shift either to a higher or to a lower gear, depending upon the instructions from the one ministering. Whenever you receive instructions from the speaker or the one ministering to do something at the last minute, respect him and submit to those instructions as he is the higher authority.

Don't complain, don't pout, don't feel inferior. Just know that the speaker hears from the Spirit of God, and there is a reason for the last-minute changes. Even in situations where you feel the instructions of the speaker are wrong, submit and obey them. If they are wrong, he will correct them later, if necessary.

You are assigned to assist and be of help. Do your job to the best of your ability and all will go well.

Guidelines for Seating People

The first challenge you may face as the doors open is people running to get good seats. Deal gently and lovingly with these people, and guide them to the best seats that are available to them.

The second challenge is sometimes the order in which you fill certain sections of seats. Some guidelines that will help you in seating people are:

1. Fill the front rows first.

2. Have people move together (sit together) and do not leave any single seats between them.

3. Know how many seats you have in your section, and fill it from the front to the back.

4. Know how many seats you have in the first three rows. When you have three empty

seats in the first row and a party of three comes in, you will know exactly where to seat them. By knowing your sections and the availability in each, you will then be able to fill them expediently! Do not be concerned with any section other than the one to which you have been assigned.

5. After you have filled the front three rows, then do the same with the next three rows, etc.

6. As you seat from front to back, you will keep latecomers from disturbing people. All of the empty seats in the front rows will already be filled.

7. Keep open to your special sections, as they cannot always be filled in the same order as the regular sections. (This would include sections, such as those for visitors, staff, guests of the ministry, employees, deaf, blind, wheelchairs, cots, etc.)

8. There will usually be reserved seats for the ushers. However, seats are usually not reserved for spouses or special friends. You will need to go by the rules of the particular ministry or speaker.

9. There should be no seating allowed in the first three rows or on the side front sections for babies and small children. This is especially important when TV video taping is being done.

10. Attempt to get to know the people in your section so problems can be prevented BEFORE they occur.

Removal of Hats

Have you ever noticed that men do not wear hats in a church? In 1 Corinthians 11:7, it says, *"For a man ought not to cover his head, forasmuch as he is the image and glory of God."* The Living Bible says it more clearly: *"A man should not wear anything on his head."*

Most men who wear hats in the church have either forgotten or they don't know any better. It's best to ask them as they enter the sanctuary to remove their hat. Give them Scripture if necessary. There are many ways this can be done. Use the way that best suits your personality. Also, walk in love and, whatever you do, do not offend or embarrass anyone.

Remember, it is usually better for you to ask someone to remove his hat BEFORE the minister in charge asks you to do it.

Possible Challenge Areas

Once people are seated, try to identify possible challenge areas, such as:

1. Babies that may cry. Talk to the mothers before the service so they may know where restroom and nursery facilities are located.

2. People who give indication that they may try to interrupt the service.

3. People who want to see the speaker and talk to him personally.

4. Musical instruments—especially tamborines and bells—and people who do not know how to play them.

Some problems need to be handled immediately —or avoided by preventive measures.

1. Do not allow food or drinks in the service.

2. Do not allow animals of any kind in the service. (The only exception would be seeing-eye dogs.)

3. Do not allow cameras with flash bulbs during the service. (A flash will many times cause the anointing to lift from the speaker and will bring him back to the natural realm.)

4. Be sure that hallways are always traffic-free as much as possible.

5. Running children and/or unattended children should be located and stopped.

6. Be sure that, as the head usher, your ushers team is not put in a position to counsel people. This should be discussed in one of your teaching sessions so they do not become involved in this area. They have ushering responsibilities to fulfill. Refer such people to trained and authorized counselors.

7. Be sure that ushers DO NOT pray or prophesy over people.

7
Service Responsibilities

Once the singing or worship begins, the ushers and all people working with the service need to shift into another gear. It is now time for the entire body of believers to get their minds on God the Father, the Lord Jesus Christ, and become aware of the presence of the Holy Spirit with respect and reverence.

There are many things that the ushers, hostesses or greeters, and the ones leading the music can do to create a worshipful atmosphere.

During the worship, praise, and prayer portions of the service, the ushers should spread out around the walls and get involved with the service. As an usher, you are part of the service, and your actions will affect the service.

You can help the people on the platform as follows:

- If they are singing—sing.

- If they are clapping—clap.

- If they are laughing—laugh.

- If they are dancing—dance.

- If they are jumping—jump.

- If they are weeping—weep.

- If they are praising God—praise God.

Don't stand around like wooden soldiers. Be sincere. Don't fake it. You may have to start in the flesh, but you will quickly be caught up in the Spirit as you join in with the activities of the service. Remain alert to your duties, however, as you continue to welcome and seat the people until the worship begins. You will need to keep your eyes open as you worship since your duties have just begun. You are expected to worship and to get involved in the service, but you must remain alert with your eyes open. If you close your eyes, you may miss any one of the following situations:

1. The speaker may be trying to get your attention.

2. The musicians may be trying to get your attention.

3. A situation may be developing that you need to take care of immediately.

4. There may be someone out of order who is trying to approach the platform.

5. A guest of the ministry may be arriving late.

6. Wheelchair or cot patients may come in late and need your direction to find their designated area for seating.

What To Do When the Speaker Is Late

When the singing has been completed and the speaker has not yet arrived, you may be able to proceed with one of the following:

1. Have a testimony from each section.

2. Sing more songs.

3. Be ready to preach or teach yourself.

Seating People During the Singing Portion of the Service

The first part of the service usually involves singing, worship, praise, and prayer. Many times singing is used to get people in their seats so the service may begin. Music should not be used in this way, but with some congregations it may be mandatory.

During the first phase, the music is usually more outgoing, such as with the clapping of hands or movement of feet. It is used to create an atmosphere of peace and well-being, as many of the people who have come into the service have rushed around in their daily routines and are still uptight.

During this time, it is still permissible to seat people. At this stage of the service, the people are usually happy, friendly, and are free to greet one another.

Seating During the Worship and Praise Portion of the Service

The tempo of the service will begin to change as the music is changed to worship as unto the Lord. This type of singing will normally go into praise and singing in the Spirit, many times followed with prophecy and prayer.

During the worship, praise, and prayer portions of the service, **DO NOT SEAT ANYONE**. Latecomers should be held at the doors until this part of the service is concluded.

Some of the reasons why you need to hold the people at the doors and control the movement at this time are:

1. It is difficult to worship the Lord when people are stepping on your toes, or when they are tapping you on the shoulder to ask you to move so they can be seated.

2. When people realize that they can worship with their total attention on Jesus, there is more freedom to worship; and it lays the groundwork for a higher level of praise.

Seating People Once the Service Has Begun

The following suggestions should be helpful in seating people once the service has begun:

1. Seat people near the front during the opening songs if there are any seats left at the front. (Front seats, as discussed earlier, should always be filled first.)

2. DO NOT seat people during the worship and praise portions of the service.

3. DO NOT allow movement during messages in tongues and interpretation or prophecy. (This is a very sacred time, and distractions must not be allowed.)

4. Never just stand and watch when people come into the service, whether the service has begun or not. Immediately move to help people.

5. When people are held at the doors during these special times of worship, they should not be seated until the ushers receive a signal from the head usher that it is now permissible to do so.

    a. Do not let the people take their seats until the second phase of the service or until the head usher has given the signal.

b. Normally there will be a release in your spirit when it is permissible to seat the people; however, it is still best to wait for the signal from the head usher.

c. When you have latecomers in walkers or older people who find it difficult to stand, attempt to seat them near the back if seats are available.

6. During prayers, altar calls, and offerings, the same procedures should be followed in stopping people from entering the services. At the conclusion of each of these portions of the service, they may be seated.

Handling Possible Interruptions of Crying Babies During the Service

The following guidelines will help alleviate most of the interruptions that usually occur during a service:

1. Order must be maintained in the service at all times to avoid weakening or interrupting the flow of the anointing of God on the one ministering.

   "Let all things be done decently and in order" (1 Corinthians 14:40).

2. To prevent interruptions during the service, it is important to intercede before and during the service. Speak the spirit of peace into manifestation, and rebuke any spirits of disruption.

3. Sometimes it will be necessary to give a warning to parents who do not attempt to quiet their children during the service, who have children standing in their chairs, who have children turned around, or who have children with noisy and distracting playthings.

4. Do not remove a parent with a disruptive child unless the Spirit of God tells you to do so.

   a. You must remove the parent and child if the platform is being disturbed.

   b. You must remove the parent and child if people sitting nearby are being hindered from receiving.

   c. You must remove the parent and child if they have been warned to be quiet and do not follow the directive given. If you have warned them once, insist that they move to an alternate area as quietly and quickly as possible.

d. When you remove someone, do it quietly and pleasantly. Attempt to minister to all of the people in the area, not just parents and baby.

1) Wait in back while parent gathers belongings.

2) Don't create a hostile atmosphere.

3) Avoid feelings of anger.

4) Avoid projecting condemnation.

e. Should the parents refuse to leave, don't force the situation; contact the head usher.

f. When you escort someone out, be courteous:

1) Open all doors.

2) Escort the parent and child all the way to the alternate area.

3) Project an attitude of appreciation.

4) Don't apologize or act defensive.

5) Give reasons for removal only if questioned or if you sense tension. (Explain that others are not used to noise nor can they receive when noise prevails.)

6) When back in the main room, check vacated area for dropped or forgotten items. Don't remove personal items.

7) Report any problems or confrontations to the head usher after the service.

(A handout on "CRYING BABIES" is found in Appendix 2 on pages 126-127.)

Taking Pictures During the Service

There should be no picture taking (other than the regular televising of the service) during the service, other than what is appointed by the speaker himself. There are several reasons for this.

1. Flash bulbs many times disturb people in the congregation.

2. When flash bulbs go off, they sometimes cause the anointing to lift from the speaker.

3. The moving about with the picture taking is sometimes distracting. (People will many times watch the photographer and will not hear what the speaker is saying.)

4. Only one person, if any, approved by the one ministering will be allowed to take pictures. All others will be asked to keep their seats.

5. No one will be allowed to go on to the platform to have their pictures taken.

6. A 35 millimeter camera will usually be allowed as long as the people using it remain in their seats.

Responsibilities of Ushers in the Back of Auditorium

Ushers in the back of the auditorium must remain alert at all times, pray in the Spirit continually, and be of help in the following areas where possible:

1. Open and close the doors for people, especially for the latecomers, for those leaving early, to avoid slamming or squeaking of the doors which can be very distracting.

2. Be responsible for handling these areas:

    a. Latecomers.

    b. People looking for the nursery.

    c. Hallways.

    d. Lobbies.

    e. Messages for the platform (give to head usher if possible).

    f. Counting of number of people at the meeting.

    g. Watching and assisting with any movement or activity during the service.

    h. Remaining alert to actions during the service.

    i. Controlling the thermostats.

8
Offering Procedures

Before the offering is taken, you need to know:

1. What section are you assigned to?

2. Do you pass the buckets or do you pick them up?

3. Where do you stand?

4. When do you pass out visitor's cards or packets?

5. When do you pass out envelopes?

6. How do you know when to pass the offering buckets?

7. Where do you go with the offering once it has been collected?

8. Do you help count the offering?

9. When do you return to your seat?

If you do not know the answers to these questions, even though they are simple ones, you open the door for doubt and confusion to step in. Keep those kinds of doors closed through careful and thorough planning.

Supplies Needed Before Taking Your Seat

By going through this simple checklist, you can be assured of having the proper materials for the offering and/or announcement portions of the service.

1. Count the number of rows in the section to which you have been assigned. Make sure that you have enough offering buckets for each row.

    a. Never wait until another section has taken their offering and then use their buckets for your section. (This causes embarrassment because of poor planning.)

    b. In the event you do not have enough offering buckets, always cover the front sections first, and then work your way toward the back.

2. Make sure you have the proper offering envelopes in your coat pockets.

    a. Many times a church may have a different color of envelope for different events or different fund-raising projects. Know in advance which envelopes you are to use by checking with the head usher.

    b. You may be responsible for having two or three different envelopes on you at one time. If so, make sure you know which ones to use for which offering. DO NOT GET THEM MIXED UP.

3. You may have special visitation cards or special mailing cards from the guest speaker.

   a. Be sure you have them available in your coat pockets if they are to be used. (This is the reason ushers usually wear a coat one size larger than their regular size and they keep their coat buttoned.)

   b. Never put envelopes and/or cards in your outside coat pockets. It looks sloppy and also ruins the coat.

4. You may use non-cash or promise cards on special occasions.

   a. If your church is receiving non-cash gifts, such as land, cars, and jewelry, you will, in most cases, have a non-cash card for the donor to fill out. This is for Internal Revenue Service purposes.

   b. A promise card or pledge card is used when one doesn't have the money now, but wants to give later. (Many times this is on the regular offering envelopes, but if not, a promise card is then used.)

How to Take Up the Offering

The following guidelines help to take up the offering most expediently:

1. Remain in your seat or assigned position until the signal is given or the speaker says it is time to give to the Lord.

2. Then move to your aisle or assigned section.

   a. Face the front.

   b. Stand at attention and stand side by side with the other person in the aisle with you. (Usually there will be two in each aisle. He will take care of his section, and you will take care of your section.)

   c. Look sharp with coat buttoned, tie fixed, hands down by your sides; and be sure that your shirt collar is not sticking out, but is inside of your jacket.

3. Remain in an attitude of reverence until the one taking up the offering mentions that the ushers have envelopes.

   a. Don't jump ahead of the Lord. Wait until you are told to give out the envelopes.

   b. On some occasions, you may be required to stand for 20 minutes or more while the Lord is moving on the people. Simply remain standing as straight as possible; don't move around or draw attention to yourself. (Don't lock your knees—standing in a locked position for many minutes may cause light-headedness.)

4. Prepare to hand out the materials.

   a. Listen for the signal from the speaker.

   b. ALL ushers should move at the same time as a team. (If everyone is moving as a team, the offering will be taken in a very orderly manner.)

5. When the speaker asks if anyone wants an envelope, respond quietly and quickly.

   a. Turn around, face the people, hold the envelopes up in the air.

   b. Watch the people and catch their eye to see if they want an envelope.

   c. Walk all the way to the back of your aisle whether you see a hand or not. Many times a person will not raise his hand until you get right beside him.

   d. Walk back to the front.

   e. Turn around and look one more time. If you see any hands in your section, give them an offering envelope.

f. DO NOT run to another section when you see a hand raised. Your actions at this time will have a direct effect upon the offering.

g. Return to the front, and wait for the signal to pass the offering buckets.

h. All of the ushers should pass the buckets at the same time.

i. When passing the offering buckets, keep some envelopes in your hand in case someone needs one. (By having them in your hand, you won't have to stop and reach in your coat pocket to search for one.)

j. Cover your section, and trust God that the other ushers will take care of their sections.

k. One usher will be designated to collect the offering from the platform.

l. Listen to the prayer. Sometimes special instructions are given during the prayer. (You may be given special instructions to return to the platform to pray over the offering once it has been received.)

m. The offering buckets should always be passed toward the center or from front to back.

n. If you have people standing in the halls or outside during the offering, you are robbing them if you do not give them an opportunity to give. Have an usher pass an offering bucket through these areas.

o. Once the usher has finished his section, he should:

1) Remain in the back until all of the offering buckets are collected.

2) If the one picking up the buckets needs help or misses some buckets, help him out. Otherwise, wait until all of the buckets have been picked up in each section. Then all ushers with offering buckets will leave the room at the same time.

3) Make sure all of the buckets are collected and taken out of the room, including the ones not used.

4) All ushers should exit out of the same door. (This door will be designated before the service by the head usher.)

Counting the Offering

If the head usher is responsible for counting the offering, develop a system that will be expedient. The following guidelines should be helpful in assuming the responsibility of counting the offering:

1. After the money is dumped out of the offering buckets, pray over it.

2. Attempt to use the same people in counting the offerings in all of the services.

3. Always have sufficient materials on hand to count the offerings.

   a. A room with a table and chairs.

   b. Letter openers or knife.

   c. Coin separaters and counters, if possible.

   d. Coin wrappers and money binders.

   e. Deposit slips in duplicate (if this is in your area of responsibility).

   f. Calculators to figure total offering.

   g. Pencils, pens, and paper.

   h. Rubber bands and paper clips.

   i. A trash can.

   j. A briefcase with a lock for the money bag.

k. Possible security guards.

l. A safe or car to take the money to a safe.

4. Assign ushers specific responsibilities, such as:

a. Have one open the envelopes.

b. One will fill out envelopes for all checks that have been put in the offering without an envelope. (The envelopes are needed by the ministry for Internal Revenue Service receipts.)

c. One will straighten the bills and face them in the same direction.

d. One will separate and count the coins and roll them in the proper coin jackets.

e. Dollar bills should be counted in stacks of $25 with a paper clip on them and then a rubber band or money binder around four stacks, making a total of $100.

f. The $10, $5, and $20 bills should be put into stacks of $100 with a paper clip or money binder around them.

g. Always double check the amount of the offering with at least two people checking it.

h. The amounts of the offering must be kept confidential.

i. Never take the money home with you. Find a place to lock it up if you do not have a safe. Never assume that the ministry thinks you are honest so you can handle the money in a haphazard way. You will only be asking for trouble. (It is better to overdo the security than to allow the enemy to attack you or to create unnecessary problems because of your failure to do the job right.)

j. Always wash your hands when you are finished counting the offering.

5. If the ushers team is not responsible for counting the offering, they will take it to a specified area where it will be put in a safe or locked up until the designated people are ready to handle it.

6. Tight security should prevail over the offering, although each church or ministry will have its own policies concerning the handling of the offering. (The location of the service and the size of the crowd will determine the amount of security needed.)

a. In large services, a uniformed security guard should be hired, not only to watch the offerings, but to stand by while the money is being counted and transported to a safe. (A security guard is also excellent in keeping people from getting out of hand during the service.)

b. Tight security practices will also discourage ushers from being tempted around the money. (The ministry must be able to trust the ushers with the offering. This is one reason ushers must be carefully selected.)

c. This is a time when the enemy will attempt to activate the spirit of theft. (Praying over the offering will give an opportunity to bind this spirit in the name of Jesus; it will also help to ensure that every penny of the offering will be used to meet the ministry's needs.)

7. All ushers should return to their designated assignments in the service at the same time when the offering procedures are completed.

  a. A signal will be given as to when to return to your seats. (This signal will usually be given so the ushers can return to their seats without disturbing the congregation, such as at the end of a song, before the speaker begins, before his opening prayer, or when the people are asked to stand. Watch the head usher for the signal.)

  b. Always be prepared for additional offerings.

  c. After carrying your buckets to the collection point (where the money is to be counted), make sure you take the same number of buckets back empty. (These can either be taken to your seat when you return or set at the rear of your section.)

8. Remember that what you are doing is "as unto the Lord." If everyone does his part, the offering will go smoothly.

9
Handling the Communion Service

There are many steps you need to take to prepare for a meaningful communion service. First, you must purchase a communion set and the communion elements. You also need to be aware of several directives that will add to the meaning of this service and about the cleaning of the set. And finally, you need to be aware of some personal preparations for the ushers that will add to the service.

In some ministries, the ushers will not be asked to assume all of these responsibilities. However, you should be alert to these steps should you be asked to handle the entire communion service.

Purchasing a Communion Set

There are several things to consider when selecting a communion set. Some of these considerations are:

1. How much do you plan to spend for the set?

2. Do you want a silver or gold set?

3. Do you want plastic or glass juice containers?

(Glass cups may be washed and reused, whereas plastic cups may be used once and thrown away.)

4. Do you want a set that you can add to as your congregation grows in size? (You can purchase a set that will serve 200, for example, and as the congregation grows, additional pieces of the same set may be added to the basic set.)

Most communion sets are available through Christian Bookstores. If they do not have the sets in stock, they will order them for you according to your needs.

In addition to the communion set, you will need a juice syringe to help fill the small cups. They come in two styles: plastic and glass. The glass syringe is much more accurate. It has the capacity to fill the cups approximately three times faster than the plastic syringe. If you are dealing with a large number being served in the communion service, you will perhaps prefer the glass syringe. You may even wish to purchase two of them to expedite this task.

Purchasing and Preparing the Communion Elements

There are different types of bread that may be served for communion. Most people prefer an unleavened bread, which comes in wafers or little squares. This can be baked by a church member or purchased at most Christian Bookstores.

The bread is representative of the body of Jesus Christ, broken for every believer.

The King James Version of the Bible says that Jesus took of the fruit of the vine. Therefore, most churches use grape juice which may be purchased at a grocery store. Some people, however, prefer to use wine. Some churches have wine and grape juice in the same tray so the people can choose for themselves.

In considering quantities of the grape juice needed, a 6-ounce bottle will serve 100 people; a 12-ounce bottle will serve 200 people; and a pint will serve 250 people. Some churches dilute the grape juice. Since grape juice is not extremely expensive, it is hardly worth the effort to dilute it unless you are serving thousands of people, in which case you may prefer to dilute it. Whether it is diluted or not, whether it is wine or grape juice, it is representative of the forgiving blood of the Lord Jesus Christ.

It will take an experienced person approximately one hour to prepare the communion trays for 250 people. However, if it is a person's first time to prepare communion, he should allow approximately two hours of preparation time.

The juice should be poured in the kitchen. Then the trays must be carried to the sanctuary to be placed on the communion table. Extreme caution must be used so the juice does not spill out of the cups onto the trays.

Setting up the Tables

The number of people being served communion will determine the size of the table needed to hold the communion set and elements. Be sure that you do not use a table that is too crowded. Normally, a four-foot table, draped with a white linen tablecloth, will be an appropriate size. In some churches, it is preferred to have another white tablecloth over the top of the communion set, which will be removed before the service begins.

It is best to have the juice in the center of the table with the bread at each side. In most churches, the communion will be served from the front. Therefore, everything should be completely set up before the congregation begins to arrive for the service.

General Guidelines for the Communion Service

The first decision regarding a communion service is WHEN is it to be held. Some churches have a designated Sunday each month or have designated one of the week-night services for holding the communion service. In addition, there will sometimes be special communion services, such as an Easter sunrise service, or Christmas Eve and New Year's Eve services.

In small churches, the pastor will usually handle the complete service. In larger churches, the pastor will usually delegate the handling of all arrangements to someone else.

The people who prepare the communion service need to be born again and living a life that is a pure reflection of the Lord Jesus Christ.

Some churches will use their board members as the committee to serve communion. Other churches will use their ushers. Ushers are perhaps most expedient since they are acquainted with the special directives for other types of services.

Some churches have what they call a "closed" communion. This means they will only serve members of their own assembly. If this is the case, visitors and guests will feel left out, for communion should be for all people who have been born again. If it is to be an "open" communion, which includes ALL of the people in the congregation who have been born again, this needs to be clearly stated. Every person that is present should be offered the opportunity to participate in the communion service, even the nursery workers and others who are not inside the church facility.

Many people think that young children—ages 5, 6, 7, and 8—should not be served communion, but many children are saved by the time they are 3 years of age in Word churches. Other people say that children should not be served because they won't understand the meaning of the service.

It is best to serve the communion elements to all by faith, offending no one, rather than denying someone the privilege of receiving a blessing.

Children need to be taught why we partake of communion, what it represents, and the blessing of participating in it. They need to know that grown-ups have had their sins forgiven by the blood of Jesus Christ. Children then, by participating in the communion service, are saying, "Thank You, Jesus, for forgiving my sins and saving me."

Communion should be one of the most important and sacred parts of the church service. People will be healed and some will even be saved as a result of this special service.

Procedures for Ushers Participation in the Communion Service

If certain procedures are followed, the service will be handled so quickly and beautifully that every person participating will receive from the Lord while partaking of the elements. Ushers, or those assigned to handle this service, should follow these procedures:

1. Always arrive at least 30 minutes (preferably one hour) before the doors open if you are to help with the communion service.

2. Communion may be handled in a number of ways. However, it should go like clockwork with each person doing his part, very similar to the part each person plays in taking the offering.

3. When the pastor signals, move to the front in two rows.

    a. The men to carry the bread trays should go first. After receiving their trays, they should step to one side and wait for the juice trays to be distributed.

    b. When ALL ushers have their trays, they will turn and go to their respective sections and begin passing the elements.

    c. The bread is ALWAYS given first, followed by the juice.

4. Anticipate refills; they will be at the front unless otherwise noted.

5. One team will be designated to serve the pastor and any others on the podium after all have been served.

6. One team will make sure that the sound personnel, nursery workers, musicians, and others who are hearing the service but who are unable to be in their seats are served.

7. Ushers in charge of doors will make sure there are wastebaskets at each exit at the end of the service.

Personal Instructions for Those in Charge of the Service

Much prayer, thought, and preparation should go into every communion service since it is so important.

The head usher and the total ushers team need to pray one for another for the part each will have in the communion service; then pray for the service itself.

1. Pray that the people serving are completely dedicated to the Lord.

2. Pray that every person serving is walking in instant forgiveness as a lifestyle.

3. Pray for those who will serve the communion, laying hands on them, saying, "You touch the people as an extension of the hand of Jesus—even as I am now touching you."

This type of preparation should be an encouragement to each person involved in the service to live "DAILY as unto the Lord."

The prayer for communion can be as rich as communion itself. You must expect every communion service to be "something extra special." It is not to become a ritual, but rather, it should be a blessed experience.

By taking communion, a person is really saying, "Yes, Lord, I have been washed with your blood. I have been healed by Your broken body." Many people taking communion do not fully realize what it means. However, the special touch of an excellent ushers team can bring that meaning into full manifestation!

Cleaning the Set

In cleaning a new communion set, you should allow several hours to do so. It should be wiped out with a damp, clean, nonlint cloth. The edges of the trays should be handled carefully (like record albums) because most metals today, whether they are gold, silver, or aluminum, will leave finger marks on the set. Great care should be taken to wipe those marks off.

The set should be stored in a plastic bag to keep it free of dust. If it is properly cleaned immediately following each use, it will be ready for the next service.

10
Guidelines For Ministering Supernaturally

To minister supernaturally means that you are in a service where the Spirit of the Lord is having His complete way . . . He is free to have His way!

As an usher, you need to stay in the Spirit during the entire service, as there is no way to predict the moving of the Holy Spirit. You must listen carefully to what the speaker is saying, watch constantly what he is doing, and the Lord will show you the direction that will be taken.

The one ministering will be sensitive to the direction of the Holy Spirit and will follow the guidelines as the Holy Spirit sets them forth. For example, if the one ministering is listening to the voice of the Lord, he may give an altar call for salvation at the beginning of the service rather than at the end of the service. If the Lord tells him to lay hands on someone and pray for them at the beginning of the service, he will do so.

Most churches that are obeying the Spirit of the Lord are growing by leaps and bounds. If you are in this type of church, you can surely see the necessity of praying in the Spirit at all times. And because the Lord has anointed you to minister as an usher, He will prepare you thoroughly for this position.

General Guidelines for Altar Calls

If certain guidelines are followed for altar calls, it will free the Spirit of God to have His way.

1. An altar call is one of the most crucial parts of the service. The congregation should be encouraged to remain in their seats and be in an attitude of prayer. No one should be allowed to leave at this time. When people begin to leave during an altar call, it grieves the Spirit of God. And when the Spirit of God is grieved, the anointing will lift and the miracles, signs, and wonders will be limited.

2. Ask anyone who rises to leave at this time to remain seated. Be very courteous!

3. The pastor or head usher should designate several men to assist in noting upraised hands during the altar calls for salvation, the baptism in the Holy Spirit, or for recommitment to the Lord. When the minister asks for help, respond only if you are asked specifically.

    a. In an auditorium that holds about 2,500 people, two ushers should come to the first step at the front and face the congregation when assisting the pastor.

    b. One should count half of the auditorium, and the other should count the other half, giving a total figure to the speaker.

c. Be alert. Never give double figures to the pastor.

d. If you are in a huge auditorium holding 10,000 or more people, ushers should be designated the responsibility for counting of hands during altar calls for specific sections only.

4. Unless you are assisting the pastor or head usher, remain seated. Do not be looking around. Show your reverence and pray in the Spirit. This is the greatest assistance you can give at this time to free those who need to go to the altar.

5. Be ready to minister at all times, but only when you are asked to do so.

Guidelines for a Salvation Altar Call

These guidelines will be of help in having a smooth, yet successful altar call.

1. Do not try to line the people up. Let them stand in a group.

2. Do not look around. Keep your gestures to a minimum.

3. Unless you are an authorized counselor, remain in your seat when the counselors are called.

4. One usher should check the prayer or counseling room before the service begins. If this is not possible, check it right before the people are taken to this room for prayer and counseling.

   a. Be sure it is unlocked.

   b. Be sure the condition of the room is conducive to prayer and counseling.

   c. Be sure lights and air or heat are on.

   d. Be sure that proper handout materials are available.

5. If you are the usher assigned to lead the people out with the counselors, be sure that all of the people stay together. If you see one

return to his seat, gently and lovingly encourage him to go with the group.

6. Be sure that all doors are open and that you have a sufficient number of ushers to clear the way for this group of people to go directly to the prayer and counseling room.

7. One usher should be assigned inside the counseling room door and one outside the door to keep spectators away. Ushers will remain at these doors until the counselors leave.

8. Only designated and qualified counselors will be counseling.

Basic Guidelines for Healing Lines

The following 10 guidelines are "basics" for handling a healing line.

1. When there are small groups of people, ushers have already been designated to handle this situation.

2. For large numbers of people, lines will form on the right side. An usher will be in charge of restraining the people. In most prayer lines, the people will be placed in a single line across the front facing the minister. No one will come up the middle aisle. Two men will be responsible for catching, and one man will serve as a feeder, keeping the front in order and as full of people as possible.

3. Know your position; if you are not assigned to be a part of the healing line, stay in your seat. However, be ready and alert to help if you see the need.

4. Sense in your spirit what is going to take place (laying on of hands for the sick, for deliverance, confession, salvation, the baptism in the Holy Spirit, etc.)

5. Add your faith to the one ministering and to the congregation. It is not necessary for you to watch everyone fall; pray in the Spirit and reach out with your heart.

6. Continue to intercede throughout the ministry.

7. Be sure to watch the head usher at all times for special instructions.

8. Do not jump ahead of the minister, but anticipate what he is going to do. Let him lead you; don't get ahead of him.

9. Remain in your seat until the altar call is given.

10. When requested, an usher will step to the end of the line and turn back anyone attempting to come forward, especially those moved by sight, not by faith. (Be open to the Spirit of the Lord in this area.)

Specific Instructions During the Healing Line

There are many technicalities to be followed to handle an effective healing line.

1. Know where the people are to be lined up for the healing line.

    a. The speaker will usually direct you as to where to form the lines.

    b. Always be alert to the instructions from the platform.

    c. The line must always be filled with a continuous flow of people who are coming for healing. When the anointing is on the one ministering, you must get the people to him as quickly as possible. (When the anointing lifts, he will either stop the healing line, continue to pray for the people in faith, or call on another pastor to take over to complete the healing line.)

2. Keep the number of ushers assisting with the prayer line to a minimum, yet sufficient for the number of people who are in line. (You will need to rely on the Holy Spirit for the number of ushers needed.)

    I have found the best way to determine the number of ushers needed is to think of a bicycle wheel. The spokes hold the rim of the wheel away from the center when it is not moving. They are there, but you don't realize their function. But as the wheel begins to move, the spokes hold the wheel together to keep it from flying apart when the speed begins to build up. Then as the wheel slows down, the pressure is released off of the spokes, and they go back to a holding position.

This is the way the ushers should flow. They need to move when needed and step back when not needed.

3. Usually three ushers, at the most, will be needed at any given time on the carpet in the front while the one ministering is praying for the people in the healing line. (These ushers will help the people get up after they have been slain in the Spirit.)

4. Two ushers will be needed to catch. However, if the healing line is long, you may have need of one or two more ushers. Be flexible.

5. One usher will be needed to feed the lines and possibly two when the anointing is stronger.

6. One usher will be needed in the major aisles to block people from entering the lines when the ministry has begun or to direct them to the waiting line.

7. All other ushers who are not being used should be praying in the Spirit and must remain alert. Don't get carried away so much that you forget your responsibilities! Your responsibility is to make sure the speaker is able to minister at his best and that all people who come with a need are ministered to.

Specific Duties of the Catcher

If the catcher is aware of the following guidelines, his duties will be very easy.

1. The one catching should stay with the minister at all times. The catcher should never take his eyes off the man ministering.

2. His entire attention must remain on the one ministering. (If he has to do something else, then someone is not fulfilling his job.)

3. The one who is catching does not have the time to pick the people up, fill in the lines, or set up the lines. The catcher must remain with the one ministering at all times.

4. The catcher should continue to pray in the Spirit at all times.

5. The catcher should normally continue to wear his jacket and tie as he performs his duties. However, if multitudes of people come forward, he can remove his jacket, loosen his tie, and roll up his sleeves.

6. When people who are not in the Spirit fall, they will grab for anything or anyone. As a result, many things can happen, such as glasses being broken, wigs coming off, ties being pulled, or jackets being torn! Be alert!

7. Older people will often grab the one ministering. Help remove their hands from the speaker, or they will pull him over with them when they fall. (The people should be kept from touching the speaker's arms or hands.)

8. When a child is brought to the altar for healing, the parents should have the child stand alone if he is old enough to do so. (Many

times with small babies, the one ministering will take the child in his arms, pray, and then return the child to the parent.)

9. When a parent and child come together to the altar, quickly find out which one has come for prayer. If a parent comes for prayer, but is holding a baby or small child, an usher should take the child from the parent or have someone hold the child until the parent has been ministered to.

10. The catcher, as a normal rule, will catch everyone. One man can catch the entire healing line, but he needs one person to back him up. No one should get in front of the catcher. The backup man begins to function only when the assigned catcher cannot get to all of the people.

11. When there are breaks in the line, the catcher and the backup man may alternate. A break is when there are several people laying on the floor and the catcher has to walk around three or more people to get to the next one being prayed for. In this case, the backup man moves ahead and catches that person. Then the catcher is ready again.

12. It is a good habit for the backup man to catch the last person in the line so that the catcher has time to get to the other end and be ready to flow with the one ministering. (The speaker can walk straight across the platform, but the catcher has to step over many people and walk around to get to the other side.)

13. There must be teamwork between the backup man and the catcher.

Specific Duties of the Backup Man

As stated, the backup man is the one who assists the catcher. In most cases a good catcher can handle the entire line when people are falling under the power. But when the catcher cannot keep pace with the one ministering, it is time for the backup man to step in. The two will then function as a team.

The catcher has the hardest job physically, while the backup man has the hardest job mentally. Some of the specific duties of the backup man include:

1. He must be ready to move at all times.

2. He must be alert.

3. He must watch the catcher and the people in the line at all times.

4. The backup man must never be anxious to jump into the line, but must always be ready to assist when needed. (He must be like a cat after a mouse: never lazy or lax, but always ready to act!)

5. The backup man's main responsibility is to "support the catcher." If he is flowing with the Spirit of God, he will know when he should actually step in to help or when to remain in a support position of the catcher.

6. When a person falls under the power of God and is in the Spirit, even if he is not caught,

he will not be hurt. However, it is more courteous to keep pace with the line and catch every person.

7. When there are breaks in the line, the man who is backing up the catcher must go ahead of the catcher; then the catcher will resume his position at the next break.

8. When the backup man is having difficulty keeping pace, another usher needs to step in to support him. All of the ushers, therefore, must remain in an alert position so they are ready to step in to help when called upon to do so.

Specific Duties of the Ushers Picking up the People

The following guidelines will help those who are responsible for helping the people up off of the floor after they have been slain in the Spirit:

1. Help the people up when they are ready to get up. (No person should ever have to get up alone. An usher should always be there to assist.)

2. It is best to have two men assist the people up when you have long lines, one on each side of the line.

3. You may need to assist some back to their seats once you have helped them up.

4. If several people are getting up at the same time, other ushers may need to come to the assistance of the regularly assigned ushers.

5. The two people assigned to pick up the people need to work as a team.

6. Once the one ministering is used to working with an assigned team, the anointing will be able to flow more smoothly and completely unhindered.

7. While the healing line is still in process, never allow anyone to walk behind the person who is catching or between the one being ministered to and the one catching.

8. After the speaker has ministered to the person who came forward for healing, if the one ministered to is not in the Spirit but is just standing and praising the Lord, you must get him back to his seat as quickly as possible to make room for others coming for healing. (In most cases, a person under the power of God will not be able to move, clap, sing, kick, jump, or do other gestures. Usually when a person opens his eyes, he is ready to be helped up and guided back to his seat.)

9. Let the person remain on the floor under the power of God as long as they are truly under the power of God. Never slap a person in the face, as if you are trying to bring him out of a deep sleep or try to get the person up while he is still under the power of God. Don't interrupt God's work! In your enthusiasm, you can break the anointing and keep the person from receiving all that God has for him.

10. Be polite (not pushy) as you encourage people to return to their seats. You can simply say, "If you like, you can go back to your seat now."

11. Watch your attitude and your motivation. The lines need to be cleared, but it must be done in love. Do not detract from what God has done in each person by a hurried attitude in getting them out of the altar.

12. If a person is not in the Spirit, but wishes to stay, be polite and ask him to move out of the way so others may receive from God. Always operate in love.

13. In picking up older and heavier women, gently lift them up. Do not jerk them. Let them get up as they know best, but you be there to help and brace them as needed.

If you flow in the Spirit as you perform your duties, the result will be: excellence in your performance, thereby putting every person in a position to receive from God! Hallelujah!

Specific Duties of the Feeders

The feeders are the ushers who put the people in the ministering lines. They are also responsible for holding the lines back when the front is full and there is no place for the rest of the people to stand.

A feeder must know how to screen people. That is, he must make sure the people coming to the altar are coming for the specific thing the minister has stated. As an example, if the one ministering calls for the people to come to the altar who have cancer in the upper part of their body and someone comes to receive a greater anointing on his ministry, this person must be asked to wait. If you are "screening" the people properly, only those that the minister has requested will go forward. Otherwise, you will have chaos, and the anointing of God will lift from the one ministering.

The feeder needs to move people into the healing lines to keep the lines full. The reasons for this are:

1. So the one ministering can move as quickly as possible to get to as many people while the anointing is the strongest.

2. With many ministers, the anointing will only last for a specific period of time.

The one ministering would become upset, and rightfully so, if the anointing is strong and the people seeking the Healer are not put in the lines as quickly as they should be. The one ministering should never have to direct the healing line nor should he have to request those in lines to come forward to receive.

Therefore, if you are doing your job well, the speaker will be able to stay in the spiritual realm, and the anointing will remain strong. Great and mighty miracles will be the result!

How to Handle Physically Handicapped People

Anyone who is very slow in walking, is not able to stand, is in a wheelchair, or is using a walker, should be put at the end of the healing line unless the one ministering requests that they come forward.

The minister will usually go to these people once they are brought forward. By stopping the people on the end and allowing others to go around them, the lines will be filled much quicker.

You must obey the wishes of the one ministering and let the Spirit of God be your guide in handling any of the special cases.

Handling Disturbances in the Healing Line

Not all people are moved by the Spirit of God who come to the altar for healing. Those who are moved with emotionalism will quickly grieve the Spirit of God if they are not dealt with immediately. For example, some may begin praising the Lord loudly rather than with reverence and quietness; some may begin to dance at the altar, interrupting the flow of the Spirit of God. Some may begin to shout loudly.

You must deal with them quickly, remove them from the altar, and quietly and lovingly usher them back to their seats.

11
Post-Service Responsibilities

Once the service is over, you need to respect the privacy of the speaker and assist him to the speaker's room, to his car, or wherever he prefers to go.

When the speaker is ministering under the supernatural anointing of God, he has an unusual amount of strength; but when the anointing lifts, he is back in the natural realm and is usually very tired and sometimes at the point of exhaustion. This is the reason many ministers want to leave immediately when they are finished with the service. They do not mean to be rude or impersonal, but because of being wet from perspiration and physically drained, they want to be by themselves or with their own small group of people.

Many speakers do not eat before the service. They wait on the Lord in a partial fast. Then when they finish the service, they are hungry and want to eat dinner, even though it may be midnight or later in some cases.

After some services, the speaker is still so much in the Spirit realm that all you can do is put him in his car and drive him home or to his motel room. In some cases, the anointing may remain on the speaker for as long as three or four days. If this is the situation, he will still need assistance to go to his destination.

These are some of the reasons that speakers do not wish to fellowship with the congregation once the service is over. It is then up to the ushers to keep people from bothering the speakers. However, the ushers must respect the wishes of the speaker. If he wants to fellowship with the people, simply stand by to assist him. Stay out of his way, yet remain "at hand" in case he needs your help.

Final Responsibility of the Ushers

Some of the final responsibilities of the ushers, once the speaker has been taken care of, include:

1. Greet those who have come to the service for the first time and invite them back.

2. If there are still any people under the power of God, wait to assist them in getting up.

3. Assist the people with the book tables in covering them or in tearing down and repacking the books should this help be needed. If an inventory is needed, help take it quickly and efficiently. (You may need to do this for both the ministry's book table and for the book table of the speaker.)

4. Be alert to people with demonic spirits who still are in need of counseling. Direct them to the counselors.

5. If the offering is yet to be counted so the speaker can receive a check before he leaves, assist in this area.

6. If all of the counselors are gone and someone wants to be saved, it is your opportunity to lead someone to the Lord.

7. If there are lost and found items, take them to the designated area.

8. When people clear your designated **area**, straighten the chairs and pick up the trash.

9. Replenish the offering buckets in your section if this has not already been done.

10. Sometimes wheelchair patients come in faith to the meeting and need someone to take them home. Assist in this area if you **are** needed.

11. Remove water from the platform.

12. Shut down the air-conditioning or the **heat**.

13. Check the restrooms for anyone who is left there; then shut off the lights.

14. Shut off the sound system.

15. Shut off the cameras.

16. Once people are gone, shut off the lights to the parking lot and to the building.

17. Shut off the coffee pot in the speaker's room. Clean up the speaker's room as needed.

18. Be sure that the offerings and the book table money are locked in the proper places.

19. You may need to help stranded motorists in the parking lot, such as people with flat tires, stalled cars, ice on windows, etc.

20. No one should be allowed to play, touch, or use the sound equipment or any of the musical instruments, unless authorized or unless the instruments belong to them personally. (People should be discouraged from practicing on the musical instruments, as it will tend to keep people from wanting to leave the service.)

21. No one should be allowed to play the piano or organ unless authorized by the pastor or the ministry. (This also should be discouraged after the service.)

Final Comment

This book is by no means complete with ALL of the guidelines and techniques for every area of ushering. However, it is an attempt to share some of the "basic" guidelines with ushers today and to serve as an encouragement for all ushers to come into a "oneness"—which sets the pace for a mighty outpouring of the work of the Holy Spirit!

If you have mastered the ushering techniques contained herein, you are well on your way to USHERING IN HIS EXCELLENCE!

Appendix 1
USHERS APPLICATION FORM

SAMPLE

USHERS APPLICATION FORM

Name_____Home Phone_____

Birthdate_____ Business Phone_____

Address _____

Height_____ Weight_____ Jacket Size_____

Marital Status: _____Single   _____Married

_____How many children do you have?

Are you born again?_____ If yes, when?_____

Have you received the baptism of the Holy Spirit?_____

If yes, when? _____

How long have you lived in (your town)? _____

Do you consider (your church name) your church home?

_____

Are you a student?_____ If yes, name of school_____

_____

Are you or have you been active in Christian work?_____

Are you or have you ever been in the full-time ministry?_____

If yes, what were your duties and responsibilities?_____

_____

Which services (of the following) can you regularly attend?

_____Sunday, 8:30 a.m.   SEMINARS:

_____Sunday, 10:00 a.m.

_____Sunday, 11:30 a.m.   _____Thursday, 7:00 p.m.

_____Sunday, 7:00 p.m.   _____Friday, 7:00 p.m.

_____Wednesday, 7:00 p.m.   _____Saturday, 7:00 p.m.

Do you feel a definite call into the ministry of helps?_____

Have you served as an usher before?_____If so, where?

_____

For how long? _____

What do you consider your strong points?_____
_____

_____

Do you smoke? _____
Do you drink?_____
Do you use illegal drugs?_____

As an usher, we will desire you to be PROMPT, arriving one hour before the service for prayer, teaching, and preparation. We also desire that you be available for special services and seminars.

If you are scheduled to usher and cannot make it, you must give the head usher at least three (3) days notice. If an emergency arises, contact the head usher as soon as possible.

Appendix 2
HANDOUT MATERIAL—
"CRYING BABIES"

I. ATTITUDE

  A. Keep order in the service (1 Corinthians 14:40—"Let all things be done decently and in order").

  B. Prevent interruption of anointing.

  C. Help those near the baby to receive.

  D. Help the parents of the baby to receive.

II. PREVENTION

  A. Intercession: before and during meeting.

  B. Release of faith—speak the spirit of peace into manifestation.

  C. Rebuke any spirits of disruption.

  D. Placement: near the back or on an aisle.

III. WARNINGS

  A. Parents not attempting to quiet a child.

  B. Children standing in chairs.

  C. Children turned around.

  D. Noisy or distracting playthings.

IV. REMOVAL

  A. When to remove
    1. Listen to your spirit.
    2. Before the platform is disturbed.
    3. Disturbing those near the baby.
    4. Parents not attempting to quiet a baby.

  B. Technique
    1. Be pleasant.

2. Remember: minister to the area, not just to the parent and baby.

3. First trip

   a. SUGGEST alternate area.

   b. If they want to stay, instruct that they MUST stop the disturbance.

4. Second trip

   INSIST on alternate area.

5. Be as quick as possible.

6. Wait in back while parent gathers belongings.

7. Don't create a hostile atmosphere.

   a. Avoid feelings of anger.

   b. Avoid projecting condemnation.

8. If parents refuse to leave

   a. Don't force the situation.

   b. Contact the head usher.

V. HALLWAY

   A. Be courteous—open all doors.

   B. Escort all the way to alternate area.

   C. Project attitude of appreciation.

   D. Don't apologize or act defensive.

   E. Give reasons for removal only if questioned or if you sense tension. (Explain that others are not used to noise.)

   F. When back in main room, check vacated area for dropped or forgotten items.

   1. Carry only misplaced items.

   2. Don't remove any personal items.

   G. Report any problems or confrontation to the head usher after the service.